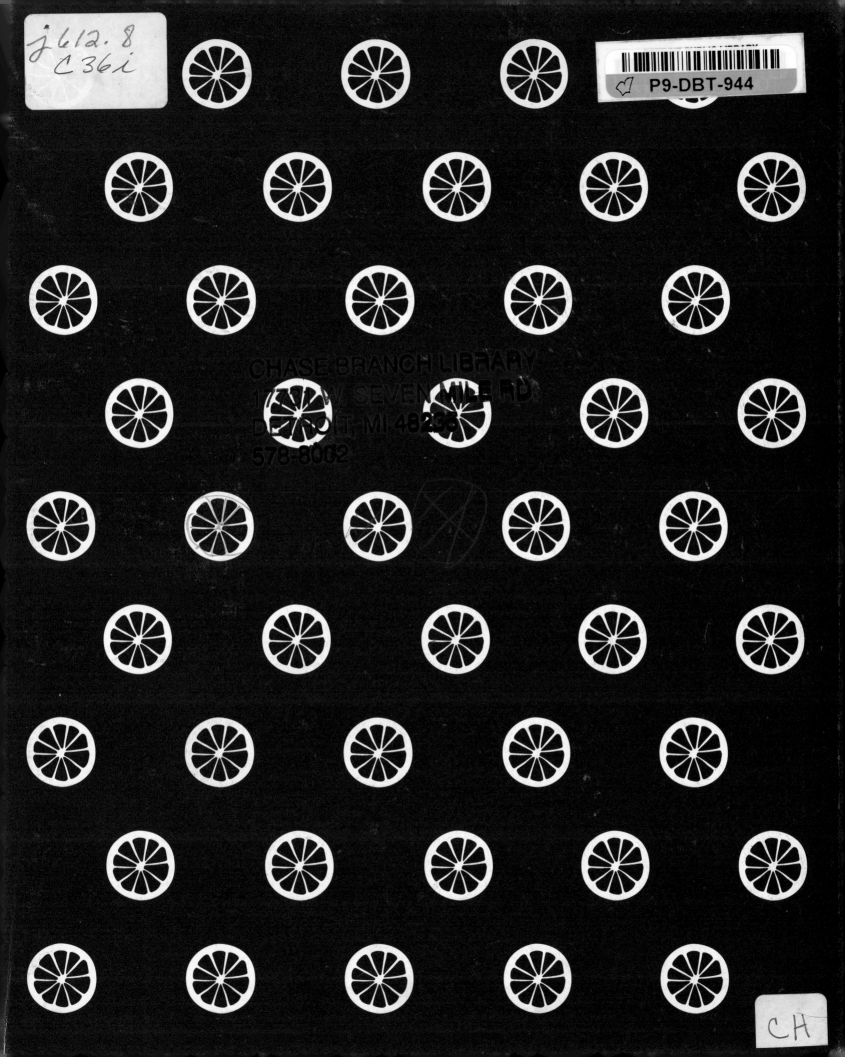

j 612. 8
C 36 i

P9-DBT-944

CHASE BRANCH LIBRARY
17731 W. SEVEN MILE RD
DETROIT, MI 48235
578-8002

CH

I Wonder Why

Lemons Taste Sour

and Other Questions About Senses

Deborah Chancellor

KINGFISHER

BOSTON

KINGFISHER
a Houghton Mifflin Company
  imprint
222 Berkeley Street
Boston, Massachusetts 02116
www.houghtonmiffllinbooks.com

First published in 2007
10 9 8 7 6 5 4 3 2 1

1TR/0307/SHENS/RNB(RNB)/126.6MA/F

Copyright © Kingfisher Publications Plc 2007

All rights reserved under International and
Pan-American Copyright Conventions

LIBRARY OF CONGRESS CATALOGING-IN-PUBLICATION DATA
Chancellor, Deborah.
  I wonder why lemons taste sour and other questions
    about the senses / Deborah Chancellor. —1st ed.
      p. cm.
  1. Senses and sensation—Juvenile literature. I. Title.
  QP434.C44 2007
  612.8—dc22
                              2006022519
ISBN 978-0-7534-6088-7

Senior editor: Belinda Weber
Coordinating editor: Caitlin Doyle
Art director: Mike Davis
Designer: Jack Clucas
DTP manager: Nicky Studdart
DTP operator: Claire Cessford
Artwork archivist: Cee Weston-Baker
Production controller: Teresa Wood
Illustrations: Martin Camm 8–9, 12, 15, 16–17, l20–21,
23br, 26–27, 28, 29br; Roger Stewart 4–5, l6–7, 9tr, 9br,
10–11, 13, 14, 16bl, 17br, 18–19,
21br, 22, 23tr 30–31. Peter Wilks (SGA) all cartoons.

Printed in Taiwan

CONTENTS

How do I know what's going on?

You have five different senses. These are sight, hearing, touch, smell, and taste. Each one of your senses is very important. Together, your senses tell you what you're eating, listening to, feeling, seeing, and touching.

● Your senses help you understand the world around you. They warn you about danger, but they also help you enjoy things, like music.

● Some people say that they can "feel" something happening, even though they can't see, hear, smell, taste, or touch it. They call this feeling their "sixth sense."

brain

spinal cord carries
messages between
nerves and the brain

Can senses get on my nerves?

Your senses cannot work without your brain. Your eyes, ears, nose, tongue, and skin send messages to your brain through your body's nervous system. Your brain then tells you how to react.

Why are polar bears great detectives?

Animals have amazing senses. For example, a polar bear can smell prey 12 miles away. That means that it will have to run as far as half a marathon to catch its next meal!

Why is my tongue bumpy?

Your tongue is covered with small bumps called taste buds. When you take a mouthful of food, your taste buds send a message to your brain. This helps you identify the taste and decide if you like it. Many people like sweet things, like cotton candy.

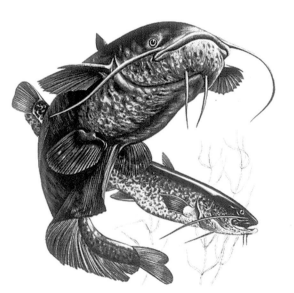

Why is a catfish like a tongue?

Catfish have taste buds all over their bodies, even on their long, whiskery barbels. These help them find food in the muddy, murky water in which they live.

• Blowflies taste with their feet! Their feet are covered with special hairs that taste the food when they land on it. If they don't like the flavor, they just fly away.

Do girls taste better than boys?

Most people have around 10,000 taste buds inside their mouths. If you are a girl, you have more taste buds than most boys have. Your taste buds are mostly on your tongue, but some taste buds are on the roof of your mouth.

• Most vegetables, such as spinach, have a bitter taste. Many children do not like this taste, but these vegetables are very good and healthy to eat.

How fussy is a koala?

The koala is the world's pickiest eater. It will only eat eucalyptus leaves, and it spends most of its day searching for exactly the right type. Most other animals, including people, eat many different things.

- Your sense of taste stops you from eating things that could make you sick. Rotten apples taste bad—so you want to spit them out before you swallow them.

- The monarch butterfly is the sweet-tooth champion of the animal world. It is more than 1,000 times more sensitive to sweet flavors than you are!

How do I taste with my nose?

Your sense of smell is connected to your sense of taste. When you have a cold, your nose gets stuffed up, and you can't smell things very easily. This means that you can't taste your food very well until you get better.

● Thousands of years ago sweet foods, such as honey, were hard to find. Whenever our ancestors found something sweet, they ate it right away. They developed a sweet tooth, which many of us still have today.

Why do lemons taste sour?

Lemons contain citric acid, which tastes sour. You pick up this flavor along the sides of your tongue. The lemon taste is so strong that you can tell if one drop of lemon has been mixed with 50,000 drops of water!

Which dogs sniff for trouble?

A dog's sense of smell can be up to one million times more sensitive than a human's. This is why the police and customs officers train dogs to sniff out and find hidden drugs and explosives. Police also use dogs to help them find missing people.

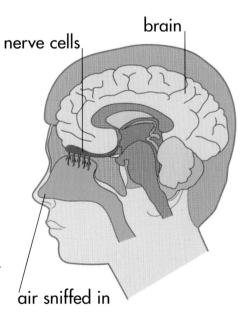

How does my brain smell?

● When people are scared, their sweat contains a special chemical. This could be why dogs and horses can smell if someone is frightened. This is bad news for cowardly cowboys!

When you sniff, air moves around inside your nose. Nerve cells recognize the smells and send signals to your brain, which tells you what you are smelling.

nerve cells

brain

air sniffed in

How do I escape from bad smells?

Smells tell you if things are good or bad. They can warn you about danger such as poisonous gases in the air. You can then move away from the smell before it makes you sick.

● Smells trigger the emotional part of your brain and can remind you of good or bad things. Nice smells, like a freshly baked cake, can make you happy, while bad smells can make you angry.

● Animals use smells to mark their territories, warn off predators, or attract a mate. Some male moths can smell a female moth from almost two miles away. It would take you about half an hour to walk that far.

Why does a skunk stink?

The skunk is the world's stinkiest animal. If it is threatened by a predator, such as a bear, the skunk sprays a smelly, sticky fluid at its attacker's eyes. The liquid smells so bad that it can make the attacker sick, allowing the skunk to escape.

● Mosquitoes are attracted to humans by their smell. They especially like the smell of hot, sweaty feet!

Do I smell more than my mom?

When you are young, your sense of smell is at its best. You can tell the difference between 4,000 to 10,000 smells. As you get older, you can detect less smells. So, yes, you can smell more than your mom!

● Some smells bring back memories. The smell of popcorn can make you think of your favorite movie. This is because your sense of smell is connected to the part of your brain that deals with emotions.

What's that smell?

You react quickly to smells—some are nice, but others are disgusting! There are four main types of smells: fragrant (like roses), fresh (like a pine tree forest), spicy (like cinnamon), and putrid (like rotten eggs).

When is it good to feel the heat?

You have millions of touch receptors right beneath your skin. They send signals to your brain, which tells you what to do next. For example, your brain tells you to move away from a fire before it burns you.

● You don't have any nerves in your hair or fingernails, so it doesn't hurt when you cut them.

How does a ladybug tickle my finger?

Your fingertips are the most sensitive part of your body. You have around 100 touch receptors in each fingertip. This means that you can feel a tickle on your skin when a ladybug moves, even if it only moves one thousandth of an inch.

● When you first get dressed, you can "feel" your clothes. Your touch receptors quickly get used to the feeling of your clothes and stop working. This is why you might forget to take off your socks before you get into the bathtub!

Which mole uses a star to find its food?

Some animals rely on their sense of touch. The star-nosed mole can't see very well, but it uses its sense of touch to find food. It has 100,000 nerve fibers between its nose and its brain. This is almost six times more than you have in your hand.

How cool are a dog's pants?

Like many animals, a dog pants in order to stay cool. It may also move into the shade or splash around in some water to escape from the heat.

● The desert iguana must lay her eggs when the sand is at the right temperature—otherwise they won't hatch. This smart lizard can tell how hot the sand is to within around one degree.

Why do I chatter when I'm cold?

When you're cold, your muscles contract quickly in order to try to warm you up. We call this shivering. Your teeth chatter as the muscles in your jaw move.

● The woodland frog lives in the Arctic, where temperatures drop far below freezing. This hardy animal can survive being frozen solid!

Why is it easy to burn my tongue?

Your tongue is very sensitive to touch, but it is not as good at telling how warm or cold food is. If you eat something that is very hot, your tongue may get burned before you feel the heat.

Why does pain mean STOP?

Pain is a warning to your body. Usually if you feel pain, you need to stop doing something or move away from something that is hurting you. When you twist your ankle, the pain warns you to stop before you hurt yourself even more.

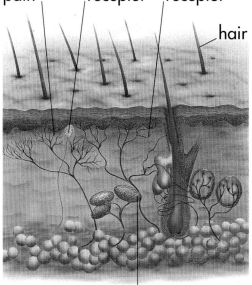

receptor for heat, cold, or pain

light pressure receptor

light touch and pressure receptor

hair

heavy touch receptor

Why do I feel pain so quickly?

Your sense of pain works very fast. This is because you have more pain receptors under your skin than any other type of touch receptor. Every square inch of your skin is packed with around 400 pain receptors.

● If you touch something sharp, like a cactus, your brain reacts so quickly that you pull away from whatever is hurting you, sometimes before you've even noticed.

When does ice cream hurt?

When something cold touches the roof of your mouth, it triggers a headache. Nerves feel the cold and widen blood vessels to try to warm up the brain. Luckily, the pain only lasts around 30 seconds.

Can dolphins make long-distance calls?

Sound travels underwater, just like it travels through air. Dolphins can communicate with each other over very long distances under the sea. Their sense of hearing is much better than yours.

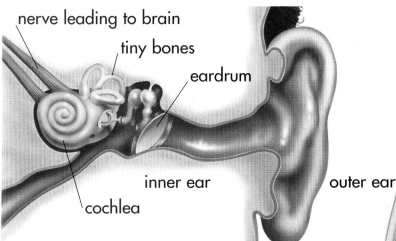

nerve leading to brain

tiny bones

eardrum

inner ear

cochlea

outer ear

Which drum helps me hear?

You have a drum inside each ear! A thin piece of skin, called an eardrum, wobbles when you hear a sound. The vibrations are carried through tiny bones to a spiral tube called the cochlea. Your brain picks up messages from the cochlea so that you can recognize the sound.

• Children have more sensitive hearing than adults have. This is why you can hear many more sounds than your grandparents can.

● Snakes do not have ears, but they can hear. They pick up vibrations with their scales, muscles, and bones. Inside their head, an inner ear hears the sounds.

Are two ears better than one?

You have two ears so that you can figure out where a sound is coming from. A sound reaches each one of your ears at a slightly different time. This helps you know whether the sound is coming from the right or the left.

How do my ears stop me from falling?

Your ears are not just listening machines. You can keep your balance because of what goes on inside your inner ear. Gymnasts have very good balance and can perform exercises on a balance beam.

- When you are in a car, your senses can get confused. Your eyes focus on something that is still inside the car, but your inner ear detects that you are moving. This can make you feel very sick.

- An elephant's big ears are very useful on a hot day. They flap like fans to cool down the animal.

What liquid makes me feel dizzy?

When you spin around, liquid in your inner ear spins around, too. When you stop moving, it also takes a while for the liquid to stop moving. This is why you can feel dizzy for a while.

• If you climb a mountain or go high up in an airplane, the air pressure changes. This affects your eardrums and makes your ears pop.

Which animal is batty about echoes?

Bats have the best hearing of all land animals. A bat makes high-pitched sounds, which hit its prey and then bounce back. From this echo, the bat can figure out how big the prey is, how fast it is moving, and where it actually is.

Is sound speedy?

Sound travels through the air at around 760 miles per hour. Light travels much faster, so sometimes you see things before you hear them. If you watch a space shuttle launch from far away, you will see the blast before you hear the noise.

● If you blow a dog whistle, dogs will hear the sound, but you won't. This is because the whistle has a very high frequency, which you can't hear.

● Some singers can shatter glass. If they hit exactly the right note to make the glass vibrate and then increase the volume, the glass will wobble so much that it breaks.

How loud is a whale's whistle?

The blue whale makes a whistling sound. This amazing noise measures up to 188 decibels, which is as loud as a space rocket launch!

● Huge telescopes pick up radio signals from outer space. Astronomers listen carefully to these signals. They hope that one day they will hear a message from an alien "out there."

Which bells measure sound?

Sounds are measured in "decibels." A very quiet sound, like a whisper, is only 20 decibels. A jet plane taking off is around 140 decibels. The loudest sound ever heard was a volcano erupting. But be careful! If you listen to very loud sounds for too long, you will damage your ears and your hearing.

Which bird is eagle-eyed?

Eagles have incredible eyesight. They can see a mouse move from almost one mile away. At the back of the bird's eye there are four million light receptor cells per inch. This is five times more than you have at the back of your eye.

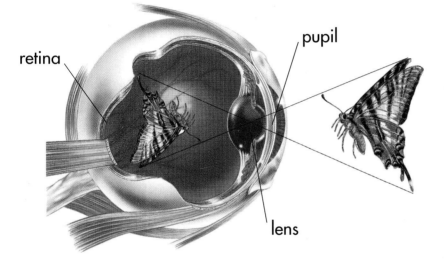

retina

pupil

lens

When is the world topsy-turvy?

When you look at an object, rays of light bounce off it and enter your eye through your pupil. These rays pass through a lens, forming an image on your retina. This image is upside-down, but your brain "sees" it as if it was the right way up.

● The world's largest telescope is at the top of Mauna Kea, a volcano in Hawaii. The telescope is eight stories high and powerful enough to see a golf ball 90 miles away!

● When babies are born, they gradually learn the difference between up and down. What they see is out of focus to begin with, but it is not upside-down!

When do your eyes grow in the dark?

You need light in order to see things clearly. In the dark your pupils get bigger to let in the small amount of light that there is.

pupil gets smaller in bright light

pupil gets larger in the dark

Can we be blinded by color?

A rainbow shows seven different colors, but you should be able to tell the difference between around eight million colors. But some people are colorblind, which means that they can't tell the difference between some colors, especially red and green.

Why do cats' eyes glow in the dark?

At the back of a cat's eye, behind the retina, is a thin tissue that reflects light and helps the cat see better. Cats open their eyes wide in the dark, and their eyes reflect any small amount of light that there is.

● An ostrich's eyes are bigger than its brain!

● The pygmy tarsier may be tiny, but its eyes are huge compared to its body. If your eyes were this large compared to your body, they would be as big as grapefruits!

Why is a dog's life gray?

Dogs don't have the special cells at the back of their eyes that detect color. They see the world in shades of gray.

Why do glasses help you focus?

If you are nearsighted, you can't see things that are faraway. If you are farsighted, you can't see things that are closeby. People are nearsighted or farsighted because the lenses in their eyes are not exactly the right shape. A pair of extra "lenses," either glasses or contact lenses, help them see much better.

● You blink every two to ten seconds, and each blink takes around 0.3 seconds. This means that you spend around 30 minutes every day with your eyes closed—so watch out when you're walking!

Why are bright lights blinding?

Looking at very bright light damages the light-sensitive cells at the back of your eyes. You should never look directly at the Sun, not even through sunglasses. It could make you go blind.

Why are eyebrows like a sweatband?

Your eyebrows stop sweat from running into your eyes. You couldn't function without your eyelashes, either. They keep your eyes clean and protect them from bright light.

● Crying is very good for you because it keeps your eyes healthy. The saltwater in your tears cleans your eyes and keeps them moist. Chefs who chop onions must have very healthy eyes!

● Snakes do not have eyelids, so they never shut their eyes. This means that they sleep with their eyes open!

Index

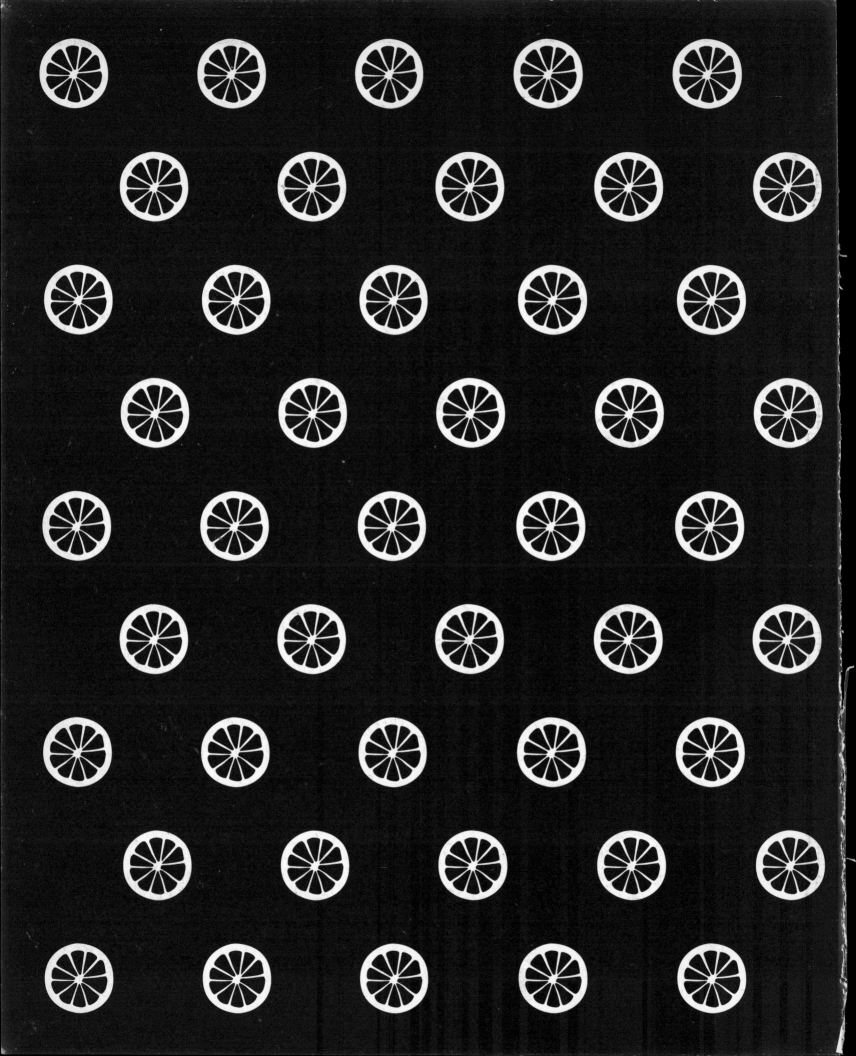